CREATING THOUSANDAIRES

A Path to Financial Security

David Runyon

Runyon Professional Publishing

CONTENTS

Title Page
Copyright
Disclaimer
Introduction
Chapter 1: Redefining Wealth — 1
Chapter 2: The Power of Consistent Savings — 4
Chapter 3: Breaking the Paycheck-to-Paycheck Cycle — 8
Chapter 4: Budgeting with Purpose — 13
Chapter 5: Investing 101 for Beginners — 19
Chapter 6: Building Multiple Streams of Income — 25
Chapter 7: Mastering the Thousandaire Mindset — 56
Chapter 8: Financial Literacy: — 64
Chapter 9: Handling Setbacks and Staying the Course — 70
Chapter 10: Celebrating the Thousandaire Milestone — 86
About The Author — 91

Copyright © 2024 David Runyon

All rights reserved

The characters and events portrayed in this book are fictitious. Any similarity to real persons, living or dead, is coincidental and not intended by the author.

No part of this book may be reproduced, or stored in a retrieval system, or transmitted in any form or by any means, electronic, mechanical, photocopying, recording, or otherwise, without express written permission of the publisher.

Cover design by: Haley Vic
Library of Congress Control Number: 2018675309
Printed in the United States of America

DISCLAIMER

Creating Thousandaires: A Path to Financial Security is intended to provide general financial information and insights based on the author's knowledge and experiences. This book does not constitute financial advice or legal advice, nor does it substitute for professional guidance from licensed financial advisors, tax professionals, or legal experts. Readers should consult with a qualified financial professional before making any significant financial decisions to ensure that they are acting in accordance with their own unique financial circumstances, goals, and risk tolerance.

All information in this book is provided "as is," with no guarantee of completeness, accuracy, timeliness, or outcomes. The author and publisher disclaim any liability arising from any use or reliance on this information. Financial markets, economic conditions, and legal regulations are subject to change, and past performance is not indicative of future results.

INTRODUCTION

In a world where "millionaire" is the buzzword, the goal of becoming a thousandaire is often overlooked. Yet, for many people, the concept of a thousand dollars in savings, investments, or an extra thousand a month in income is far more attainable and realistic, especially when you're starting on your financial journey. This book will walk you through the steps to becoming a thousandaire—someone with a firm grasp on their finances, who can consistently build wealth in smaller, sustainable steps.

I once read that over 60% of personal bankruptcies could be avoided with an additional $500 a month of income. That statistic comes up often in discussions about financial insecurity in the U.S. The idea is that many people who end up in bankruptcy could avoid it if they had just a bit more disposable income each month. Even a modest increase like $500 a month could help cover unexpected expenses, build a buffer for emergencies, or reduce debt — all of which can prevent financial hardship from escalating to bankruptcy.

This finding highlights how close many households are to financial tipping points, where small income gaps can have large consequences. It underscores the importance of income stability, affordable credit, and accessible emergency savings for financial resilience. In the following chapters, you will hear the phrase "Emergency Fund" multiple times. The reason for this is simple: An emergency fund is a VERY important aspect of the security of being a "Thousandaire"!

The ultimate thousandaire goal? Financial security, the

confidence that comes from knowing you have resources set aside for both the planned and unexpected moments in life. This book will guide you through essential financial habits, smart budgeting, investment strategies, and mindset shifts needed to reach that first significant milestone.

CHAPTER 1: REDEFINING WEALTH

Many of us have grown up believing that wealth only starts at millions, but that's not true. Being a thousandaire means having enough financial cushion to support your life comfortably, without the stress of living paycheck to paycheck. Here, we'll explore why the goal of becoming a thousandaire is so vital and how it can be a stepping stone to larger financial goals.

Before you start your journey toward financial independence, it's crucial to redefine your understanding of wealth. For many, the idea of being wealthy often conjures images of luxury, million-dollar bank accounts, and financial freedom on a grand scale. We are led to believe that true wealth begins only when you hit the millionaire milestone. However, that perception can create a barrier to starting a financial journey, as it feels too distant or unattainable.

Wealth doesn't always need to be measured in millions. For the average person, becoming a thousandaire and having a solid financial cushion of several thousand dollars saved, invested, or working for you, or even an extra thousand a month in liquid income, can provide a strong sense of security and peace of mind. Being a thousandaire means you have enough financial resources to cover unexpected expenses, manage day-to-day living without anxiety, and work toward future financial goals. It's a life where you aren't constantly worried about the next paycheck or an unexpected bill knocking you off course.

Why Being A Thousandaire Matters

The significance of reaching the thousandaire milestone lies in its practicality. It's an achievable goal for most people, and it's often the foundation for greater wealth. When you have a few thousand dollars in savings, you gain:

Peace of Mind: Financial stress is one of the biggest stressors in modern life. Having savings to fall back on means less anxiety about emergencies like medical bills or car repairs.

Freedom of Choice: A financial cushion allows you to make choices without the pressure of financial desperation. You can take time to find the right job, pursue opportunities for personal development, or simply enjoy life a little more.

Resilience: Being a thousandaire prepares you for financial shocks. You are less likely to rely on credit cards or high-interest loans to cover sudden expenses, protecting you from the debt trap.

A Path to Greater Wealth: Hitting the thousandaire mark provides momentum. With discipline, those thousands can grow into tens of thousands and beyond, setting the stage for even larger financial achievements.

A Stepping Stone To Bigger Goals

Becoming a thousandaire isn't just about reaching one point and stopping—it's about creating a sustainable financial lifestyle that sets you up for larger milestones in the future. The skills you develop in managing, saving, and investing smaller sums of money will prepare you for managing greater wealth later on. If you learn how to save $1,000, you can learn to save $10,000. If you can invest $1,000 wisely, you'll be prepared to invest $10,000 when the time comes.

For many people, becoming a thousandaire is the first step toward financial independence. It's the proof that you can manage money, avoid debt, and steadily grow your wealth over time. It's also a much more realistic and achievable goal for most people starting out, which makes it less intimidating and more motivating.

By redefining wealth in terms of thousands instead of millions, you're taking a practical approach to financial security. The goal is not to live in luxury but to live with peace of mind, flexibility, and confidence in your financial future.

CHAPTER 2: THE POWER OF CONSISTENT SAVINGS

Saving money sounds simple, but it requires two essential ingredients: discipline and patience. It's not enough to say, "I'll start saving tomorrow." You need to create systems that make saving a part of your lifestyle, no matter how small your income is. While it may seem impossible to save when you're living paycheck to paycheck, the truth is, with a few adjustments and a solid plan, anyone can start saving and see real results over time. In this chapter, we'll break down practical methods to save, no matter how small your income may be. We'll discuss the 50/30/20 rule of budgeting, how to automate your savings, and how even saving just $5 or $10 per week can grow significantly over time. You'll learn how to build an emergency fund and the importance of "paying yourself first" when you get paid.

In this chapter, we'll explore practical, easy-to-follow methods for saving money, from simple budgeting strategies to automating your savings. You don't need to make huge sacrifices to start building financial security. Even saving small amounts like $5 or $10 per week can have a significant impact over time. It's about getting into the habit of saving and allowing your money to grow, bit by bit.

The 50/30/20 Rule Of Budgeting

A powerful tool for managing your income and ensuring you're saving regularly is the 50/30/20 rule. This is a budgeting strategy that helps you divide your income into three categories:

50% for Needs: This includes essentials like rent, utilities, groceries, and transportation. These are expenses you can't avoid, so it's important to make sure they don't consume more than half of your income.

30% for Wants: These are discretionary expenses—things that you enjoy but aren't strictly necessary for survival, such as dining out, entertainment, and shopping. By limiting this category to 30% of your income, you can still enjoy life while making room for savings.

20% for Savings and Debt Repayment: The remaining 20% should go toward savings, investments, or paying down debt. This is where you begin to build your emergency fund, contribute to a retirement account, or pay off any high-interest loans or credit card debt.

Using this rule as a guideline helps you balance your spending while making sure saving is a priority, not an afterthought.

Automating Your Savings

One of the easiest ways to ensure you're consistently saving money is to automate the process. When savings is automatic, it doesn't require constant decision-making, and you're less likely to skip it. Many banks allow you to set up automatic transfers from your checking account to your savings account on a schedule you choose—weekly, bi-weekly, or monthly.

Start by setting aside whatever amount you can afford. Even if it's just $20 a month, that money will begin to grow without you having to think about it. Over time, as your income increases or your expenses decrease, you can gradually increase the amount you're saving.

Saving Small Adds Up

If your budget feels tight, you may wonder if saving $5 or $10 a week is even worth it. But saving small amounts consistently is how habits are built and how financial progress begins. Consider this:

- Saving $5 per week adds up to $260 in a year.
- Saving $10 per week grows to $520 in a year.

These amounts may seem modest, but over time, they create a financial buffer. And once you establish the habit of saving, you'll find it easier to increase the amounts when your financial situation improves.

The key is to start where you are. No amount is too small, and the earlier you start, the more time you give your savings to grow.

Building An Emergency Fund

An emergency fund is one of the most important financial safety nets you can have. It's a reserve of money set aside for unexpected expenses like medical bills, car repairs, or sudden loss of income. Without an emergency fund, even small financial emergencies can throw you into debt or financial turmoil.

A good goal is to have three to six months' worth of living expenses in your emergency fund. This might seem overwhelming at first, but you can start small. Begin by saving $500, then aim for $1,000. From there, gradually build it up over time. The peace of mind that comes from knowing you have a financial buffer will be well worth the effort.

Paying Yourself First

One of the most effective ways to make saving a priority is by paying yourself first. This means treating your savings like a non-negotiable expense, just like rent or utilities. Instead of waiting to see if there's anything left over after bills and discretionary spending, you save first and then live on what remains.

To do this, decide on an amount or percentage of your income that you want to save, and set it aside as soon as you get paid. Automating this process makes it even easier. When you pay yourself first, you're ensuring that saving happens before anything else, making it more likely you'll hit your financial goals.

The Power Of Consistency

Saving money is less about how much you save at once and more about how consistently you do it. Small, regular contributions add up over time, and the sooner you start, the more you'll benefit from compound interest and long-term growth.

By applying the methods outlined in this chapter—budgeting with the 50/30/20 rule, automating your savings, building an emergency fund, and paying yourself first—you'll develop the financial discipline needed to steadily build wealth, no matter your starting point.

CHAPTER 3: BREAKING THE PAYCHECK-TO-PAYCHECK CYCLE

Living paycheck to paycheck is a reality for many people, regardless of income level. It's a cycle that leaves little room for saving or investing, making financial progress feel out of reach. But the good news is that with some strategic changes, it's possible to break free from this cycle, create financial breathing room, and start building wealth.

In this chapter, we'll explore how to manage your expenses, cut unnecessary costs, and develop a clear financial plan that helps you take control of your money. We'll also tackle one of the biggest barriers to wealth creation: high-interest debt. By focusing on eliminating debt and creating a plan, you can shift from surviving to thriving.

Understanding The Paycheck-To-Paycheck Trap

The paycheck-to-paycheck cycle often feels like a financial treadmill—you work hard, but your money is spent almost as soon as it hits your bank account. Rent, bills, groceries, and other expenses pile up, leaving little to nothing for savings. This can create a sense of helplessness, where any financial emergency could push you into debt.

Breaking this cycle requires a clear understanding of where your money is going and a commitment to making changes, even if they are small at first. It's about finding ways to free up money so that you can build a buffer between paychecks, eventually creating room for saving and investing.

Step 1: Track Every Dollar

The first step in breaking free from the paycheck-to-paycheck cycle is knowing exactly where your money is going. Many people have a general sense of their expenses but don't track them closely enough to spot areas where they can make changes. Start by tracking every dollar you spend for at least one month. This includes:

- Fixed expenses (rent, utilities, car payments)
- Variable expenses (groceries, entertainment, dining out)
- Unplanned expenses (emergencies, one-time purchases)

There are many tools available, from budgeting apps to simple spreadsheets, that can help you categorize your spending. Once you have a clear picture of where your money is going, it becomes easier to identify areas where you can cut back.

Step 2: Cut Unnecessary Costs

After tracking your spending, the next step is to cut unnecessary costs. This doesn't mean depriving yourself of everything you enjoy, but it does mean making conscious choices about your spending. Here are some common areas where people can reduce expenses:

Subscriptions and Memberships: Review your subscriptions

(streaming services, gym memberships, etc.) and cancel any that you don't use or need. These small monthly fees can add up quickly.

Dining Out: Eating out is convenient, but it's often more expensive than cooking at home. Try to limit dining out to special occasions and focus on meal planning to save money on food.

Impulse Purchases: Avoid impulse buying by giving yourself a waiting period before making non-essential purchases. This helps prevent emotional spending and gives you time to consider whether you really need something.

Utilities and Services: Shop around for better deals on services like internet, cell phone plans, or insurance. Often, switching providers or negotiating with your current provider can lead to significant savings.

Transportation: Consider carpooling, using public transportation, or driving less to save on gas and car maintenance.

By cutting unnecessary expenses, even small savings can add up over time. The money you save can be redirected toward paying off debt or building your savings.

Step 3: Create A Financial Plan

Having a clear financial plan is key to breaking the paycheck-to-paycheck cycle. A plan gives you direction and helps you prioritize your financial goals. Start by answering these questions:

- What are your short-term financial goals? (e.g., building an emergency fund, paying off credit card debt)

- What are your long-term financial goals? (e.g., saving for a down payment, retirement)

- How much can you realistically save each month after cutting unnecessary costs?

Your financial plan should include a budget that reflects your income and expenses, with specific goals for saving and debt repayment. It should also be flexible enough to adjust as your financial situation changes over time.

Step 4: Eliminate High-Interest Debt

One of the biggest obstacles to breaking the paycheck-to-paycheck cycle is high-interest debt, especially credit card debt. High-interest payments can eat away at your income, leaving little room for saving. To break this cycle, it's essential to focus on eliminating debt as quickly as possible.

There are two common strategies for paying off debt:

- The Snowball Method: Focus on paying off your smallest debts first while making minimum payments on the rest. As you pay off smaller debts, you gain momentum and motivation to tackle larger ones.

- The Avalanche Method: Focus on paying off your debts with the highest interest rates first, while making minimum payments on the rest. This method saves you more money in interest over time.

- Choose the method that works best for you and stick with it. As you pay off debt, you'll free up more money each month, which can be redirected toward savings and investments.

Step 5: Build A Small Cushion

Once you've cut costs and started paying down debt, the next step is to build a small financial cushion. This doesn't need to be a full emergency fund right away, but even having $500 to $1,000 set aside can make a huge difference in preventing financial setbacks.

Your small cushion acts as a buffer between paychecks, so you're less likely to rely on credit cards or loans when an unexpected expense arises. This step helps you transition from living paycheck to paycheck to having a bit of breathing room.

Step 6: Increase Your Income

In some cases, breaking the paycheck-to-paycheck cycle may require increasing your income. If you've cut costs as much as possible and still find it difficult to save, consider finding ways to bring in extra money. Some options include:

- Side Hustles: Explore freelance work, gig economy jobs, or part-time work that fits into your schedule.

- Sell Unused Items: Declutter your home and sell items you no longer need on online marketplaces.

- Ask for a Raise: If you've been in your current job for a while, consider negotiating a raise or seeking out higher-paying opportunities.

While cutting costs is important, increasing your income can accelerate your progress and give you more financial flexibility.

Conclusion: Breaking The Cycle For Good

Breaking the paycheck-to-paycheck cycle requires a combination of cutting unnecessary expenses, eliminating high-interest debt, and developing a clear financial plan. By taking these steps, you'll create space in your budget for saving and investing, ultimately building a more secure financial future.

The journey to financial stability doesn't happen overnight, but with consistent effort, you can break free from the cycle and start living with more financial peace of mind.

CHAPTER 4: BUDGETING WITH PURPOSE

A well-thought-out budget is the foundation of financial success. It's not just a list of your income and expenses—it's a blueprint for achieving your financial goals and making sure every dollar you earn is working for you. Budgeting allows you to take control of your money, so you're not left wondering where it all went at the end of each month. It helps you prioritize essential expenses, avoid overspending, and build a plan for the future.

In this chapter, we'll guide you through the process of creating a budget that works for your life, no matter your financial situation. You'll learn how to track spending, differentiate between needs and wants, and make sure every dollar has a job—whether that's paying bills, saving, or working toward your long-term financial goals.

Why Budgeting Matters

Budgeting gives you control over your financial situation. Without a plan, it's easy to spend impulsively or lose track of your expenses. A budget helps you make informed decisions about your money, ensuring that you meet your needs, avoid debt, and still have room to save for the future.

The key to successful budgeting is intention. When you budget with purpose, every dollar is assigned a specific role, whether it's paying for groceries, setting aside savings, or contributing to a financial goal like a vacation or a new car. With a budget, you know exactly where your money is going and why, giving you confidence and peace of mind.

Step 1: Know Your Income

The first step in creating a purposeful budget is to have a clear understanding of your income. This includes:

- Regular Income: Your paycheck or any consistent income streams (after taxes).

- Side Income: Money from side gigs, freelance work, or any additional sources of income.

- Irregular Income: Bonuses, commissions, or occasional earnings. While it may not be predictable, having an estimate can help you plan.

Once you know your total monthly income, you can begin allocating it to different categories.

Step 2: Track Your Spending

Before you can create a budget, you need to understand your current spending habits. For at least one month, track every dollar you spend. This includes fixed expenses like rent or mortgage payments, utilities, and car payments, as well as variable expenses like groceries, entertainment, and dining out.

You can use a budgeting app, a spreadsheet, or even a simple notebook to record your spending. The goal is to get a clear picture of where your money is going and identify any areas where you might be overspending.

Step 3: Prioritize Needs Over Wants

Once you've tracked your spending, the next step is to categorize your expenses and prioritize needs over wants. This means distinguishing between essential expenses that are necessary for your day-to-day life and discretionary spending that you can cut back on if needed. Here's how to break it down:

Needs: These are your essential expenses, including:
- Housing (rent or mortgage)
- Utilities (electricity, water, gas)
- Transportation (car payments, fuel, public transit)
- Groceries
- Insurance (health, car, life)
- Debt repayments

Wants: These are non-essential expenses that enhance your lifestyle but aren't necessary for survival, including:
- Entertainment (streaming services, movies, concerts)
- Dining out
- Shopping (clothes, electronics)
- Hobbies and leisure activities

By prioritizing needs first, you ensure that your essential expenses are covered before you allocate money to wants. This approach helps you avoid overspending in discretionary areas while still allowing room for enjoyment.

Step 4: Give Every Dollar A Job

One of the most important principles of budgeting with purpose is assigning every dollar a job. This means that every part of your income should be allocated to a specific expense or goal.

The idea is to make sure that no money is left unaccounted for, reducing the risk of impulse spending or money "disappearing" from your account.

Here's how to assign jobs to your money:

- Cover Essentials First: Start by allocating enough money to cover all your essential expenses.

- Set Aside Savings: Next, pay yourself by allocating money to your savings, whether that's an emergency fund, retirement savings, or a specific financial goal.

- Budget for Discretionary Spending: Finally, allocate money to your discretionary categories like entertainment, dining out, or shopping. Just make sure that these categories stay within the limits of your income and don't interfere with your savings goals.

This approach ensures that all your income is working toward a purpose, whether it's covering bills, preparing for the future, or enjoying life.

Step 5: Create Sinking Funds For Large Expenses

A sinking fund is a savings strategy for future expenses that are predictable but not regular. Instead of being surprised by a large bill or expense, you can set aside small amounts each month to prepare for them. Some common uses for sinking funds include:

Car maintenance
Holiday shopping
Vacations
Annual insurance premiums
Home repairs

By saving a little each month, these expenses won't catch you off guard when they arise. Include sinking funds in your budget as regular expenses, so you're always prepared for large purchases or bills.

Step 6: Adjust And Monitor Your Budget

A budget is not a one-time plan—it's a living document that should be reviewed and adjusted regularly. As your financial situation changes (e.g., a raise at work, new expenses, or a shift in priorities), you'll need to update your budget to reflect those changes.

At the end of each month, review your budget and compare it to your actual spending. Did you overspend in any category? Did you meet your savings goals? Use this review process to make adjustments for the following month.

Step 7: Make Room For Financial Goals

Beyond covering your monthly expenses, your budget should include goals for the future. Whether it's saving for a house, paying off debt, or building an emergency fund, having clear financial goals will give your budget purpose. Set specific, measurable goals and allocate part of your income toward achieving them.

For example:
Emergency Fund: If you don't have an emergency fund yet, prioritize building one with at least three to six months' worth of living expenses.

Debt Repayment: If you have high-interest debt, make paying it off a key part of your budget.

Retirement Savings: Contribute to a retirement account, even if it's a small amount at first. Over time, this can grow through compound interest.

Step 8: Stick To Your Plan And Stay Flexible

Creating a budget is only half the battle—sticking to it is where the real work begins. Be disciplined about following your plan, but also allow some flexibility. Life is unpredictable, and there will be months when unexpected expenses arise. In those cases, adjust your budget but stay committed to your long-term goals.

Conclusion: Budgeting As A Path To Freedom

Budgeting with purpose is about more than just managing money—it's about taking control of your financial future. By designing a budget that reflects your needs, goals, and values, you'll have a clear path to follow and the confidence that comes with knowing exactly where your money is going.

When you prioritize your spending, assign every dollar a job, and regularly review your budget, you'll create a financial roadmap that leads to security and freedom. It's not about restricting your spending; it's about using your resources wisely so that you can achieve both short-term stability and long-term financial success.

CHAPTER 5: INVESTING 101 FOR BEGINNERS

Once you've built a solid foundation of saving and budgeting, it's time to make your money work for you. Saving alone won't create significant wealth, especially in today's low-interest environment. To grow your money and reach your long-term financial goals, you need to invest.

Investing can feel intimidating, especially if you've never done it before, but it doesn't have to be complicated. In this chapter, we'll walk you through the basics of investing, break down different types of investments like stocks and bonds, and explore simple, low-risk options like index funds that can help you grow your wealth over time. You'll also discover the power of starting small and how compound interest can accelerate your financial progress.

Why Investing Matters

Investing is key to building wealth because it allows your money to grow faster than it would in a traditional savings account. Over time, inflation erodes the purchasing power of your money, meaning that what you can buy with $1 today will likely cost more in the future. By investing, you're not only preserving your money's value but also increasing it.

The goal of investing is to put your money into assets that generate returns, such as stocks, bonds, real estate, or mutual funds. The earlier you start, the more time your investments have to grow. Even small amounts invested consistently over time can accumulate into significant wealth thanks to the power of compound interest.

Step 1: Understand The Basics Of Investing

Before diving into investments, it's important to understand the fundamental types of investments available. Each type carries its own level of risk and potential reward, so finding the right mix for you will depend on your goals, risk tolerance, and time horizon.

1. Stocks

A stock represents ownership in a company. When you buy a stock, you're essentially purchasing a small piece of that company. If the company does well, the value of your stock increases, and you can sell it for a profit. Additionally, some companies pay dividends, which are regular payments to shareholders.

Potential Return: Stocks generally offer higher returns over the long term compared to other investments.

Risk: Stocks can be volatile. Their value can fluctuate significantly, especially in the short term.

2. Bonds

Bonds are essentially loans you give to companies or

governments in exchange for regular interest payments and the return of the bond's face value when it matures. Bonds are generally considered safer than stocks, but their returns tend to be lower.

Potential Return: Bonds offer steady, predictable income but with lower returns than stocks.

Risk: Bonds are less risky than stocks, but they're not risk-free. There's always the possibility that the issuer could default, meaning they won't repay the loan.

3. Mutual Funds

A mutual fund pools money from many investors to buy a diversified portfolio of stocks, bonds, or other assets. When you invest in a mutual fund, you're buying shares of the fund itself, rather than individual stocks or bonds. Mutual funds are managed by professionals and offer an easy way to diversify your investments.

Potential Return: Varies depending on the type of mutual fund. Some are more aggressive (stock-heavy), while others are more conservative (bond-heavy).

Risk: Mutual funds diversify your risk, but they can still be volatile depending on the assets they invest in.

4. Index Funds

Index funds are a type of mutual fund or exchange-traded fund (ETF) that track a specific market index, such as the S&P 500. Instead of trying to beat the market by picking individual stocks, an index fund buys all the stocks in the index, making it a simple, low-cost way to invest in the overall market.

Potential Return: Historically, index funds have delivered steady returns over the long term by matching the market's performance.

Risk: Index funds carry the same risks as the stock market but are generally considered safer due to their diversification.

5. Retirement Accounts (401(k), IRA, Roth IRA)

Retirement accounts offer tax advantages that help you save and invest for the long term. A 401(k) is typically offered by employers, while Individual Retirement Accounts (IRAs) are available to individuals. Roth IRAs allow you to invest after-tax income and withdraw your earnings tax-free in retirement.

Potential Return: Depends on the investments you choose within the account (stocks, bonds, mutual funds, etc.).

Risk: Retirement accounts are as safe or risky as the investments you choose within them. They're designed for long-term growth, and the tax benefits make them an essential part of any investment strategy.

Step 2: Start Small And Grow Over Time

One of the biggest misconceptions about investing is that you need a lot of money to get started. In reality, you can begin investing with small amounts and increase your contributions as you earn more or free up additional money in your budget.

Many investment platforms allow you to start with as little as $5 to $50. Even if you're investing small amounts, the important thing is to start as early as possible. The longer your money stays invested, the more time it has to grow. This is where the power of compound interest comes into play.

Step 3: The Power Of Compound Interest

Compound interest is often referred to as the "eighth wonder of the world" because of how it can dramatically accelerate your wealth-building. It's the process by which the interest you earn on your investments begins to earn interest itself. Over time, this snowball effect can turn small investments into substantial sums.

Here's an example of how compound interest works:

Initial Investment: $1,000
Annual Return: 7% (the average annual return of the stock market)
Time: 30 years
After 30 years, your $1,000 would grow to $7,612, without you adding a single penny. If you continue to invest regularly, the growth becomes even more impressive. For instance, investing an additional $100 per month would result in nearly $122,000 over 30 years.

The key to benefiting from compound interest is to start as early as possible, even if you're only investing small amounts.

Step 4: Keep It Simple With Low-Risk Investments

As a beginner, it's important to focus on low-risk, simple investment options. You don't need to become an expert or engage in complicated trading strategies to grow your wealth. Here are a few beginner-friendly approaches:

Index Funds: As mentioned earlier, index funds are a great starting point for beginner investors. They're low-cost, diversified, and easy to understand. By investing in an index fund, you're essentially buying a small piece of hundreds of companies, reducing your risk.

Target-Date Funds: These are a type of mutual fund designed for retirement savings. You choose a target retirement year (e.g., 2040, 2050), and the fund automatically adjusts its asset mix from more aggressive (stocks) to more conservative (bonds) as you approach retirement age. It's a simple, hands-off way to invest.

Robo-Advisors: Robo-advisors are online platforms that use algorithms to create and manage a diversified portfolio for you based on your risk tolerance and goals. They're affordable, easy to use, and take the guesswork out of investing.

Step 5: Stay Consistent And Avoid Emotional Decisions

Investing is a long-term strategy, and it's important to stay consistent, even when the market experiences volatility. The stock market naturally fluctuates, and there will be times when your investments lose value in the short term. However, history shows that the market tends to rise over the long term.

Avoid making emotional decisions based on market movements. Trying to time the market by buying and selling based on short-term trends can lead to losses. Instead, stick to your long-term plan, continue investing regularly, and let the power of compound interest work its magic.

Conclusion: Invest With Confidence

Investing doesn't have to be intimidating. By understanding the basics, starting small, and staying consistent, you can grow your wealth over time and achieve your financial goals. Whether you're investing in stocks, bonds, index funds, or retirement accounts, the key is to begin now. The earlier you start, the more time your money has to grow and the closer you'll get to financial independence.

In the next chapter, we'll explore how to protect your investments and ensure that your financial progress isn't derailed by unexpected events.

CHAPTER 6: BUILDING MULTIPLE STREAMS OF INCOME

To accelerate your journey to becoming a thousandaire, it's crucial to diversify your sources of income. Relying solely on one stream of income, such as a full-time job, can limit your ability to grow wealth and puts you at financial risk if that income source dries up. By building multiple streams of income, you can not only increase your earning potential but also provide yourself with greater financial security and flexibility. This chapter will cover practical ideas for creating side hustles, starting a small business, freelancing, or investing in passive income opportunities. Diversifying your income not only brings in extra money but also provides financial security in case of job loss or economic downturns.

Why Multiple Income Streams Matter

Having multiple streams of income is about more than just making more money. It's about creating financial stability and giving yourself options. If you lose your job or your main source of income is disrupted, other income streams can keep you afloat. Moreover, having several sources of income can free you from living paycheck to paycheck, allowing you to save more, invest more, and enjoy life with less financial stress.

Think of your income streams like legs of a table—if one leg collapses, the table won't fall over because the other legs still provide support. With a single source of income, you're more vulnerable to financial setbacks, but with multiple streams, you have a safety net that can protect you from unexpected events.

Step 1: Assess Your Skills And Interests

Before diving into specific ways to create additional income, it's important to assess your own skills, interests, and available time. Building extra income streams doesn't mean you have to take on a second full-time job or overextend yourself. The goal is to find opportunities that fit your life, leverage your existing talents, and offer potential for growth.

Ask yourself the following questions:
What skills do I have that others might need?
What hobbies or interests could I turn into income streams?
How much time can I realistically dedicate to a side hustle or business?
What resources (time, money, or equipment) do I have at my disposal?

Answering these questions will help guide you toward income-generating opportunities that align with your strengths and interests, making it easier to stay motivated and committed.

Step 2: Start A Side Hustle

One of the easiest ways to create an additional stream of income is by starting a side hustle. A side hustle is a flexible job or business that you do in your spare time, and it can range from freelancing to selling products online. The beauty of a side hustle is that you can start small and grow it over time, with little risk.

Here are some side hustle ideas to consider:

1. Freelancing: Turning Skills Into Income

Freelancing is an excellent way to leverage your skills and earn extra income on your own terms. If you have a marketable skill—such as writing, graphic design, coding, marketing, or photography—you can offer your services directly to clients. Freelancing platforms like Upwork, Fiverr, and Freelancer.com make it easier than ever to connect with potential clients and start earning money quickly.

Why Freelancing?

- *Flexibility and Control*: Freelancing gives you control over your schedule and the type of work you take on, making it a great option for those with other commitments.
- *Variety of Opportunities*: Freelancing platforms allow you to find work that matches your expertise and interests, from small gigs to ongoing contracts.
- *Potential for Growth*: As you build a portfolio and gain positive reviews, you can attract higher-paying clients and more complex projects.

Getting Started with Freelancing

- *Identify Your Niche*: Start by identifying which of your skills you'd like to offer. Focusing on a specific niche, such as blog writing or UX design, can help you stand out to potential clients.
- *Set Up Profiles on Freelance Platforms*: Create profiles on platforms like Upwork, Fiverr, or Freelancer.com, detailing your skills, experience, and rates. Include a

portfolio of past work if possible to showcase your abilities.
- *Bid Strategically*: When starting out, consider bidding on smaller projects to build your reputation. As you complete jobs and receive positive feedback, you can begin pursuing higher-paying opportunities.
- *Market Your Services Independently*: In addition to freelancing platforms, promote your services through social media or a personal website. Many freelancers find clients through word-of-mouth, so let friends and family know about your offerings.

Tips for Success

- *Deliver Quality Work on Time*: Reputation is key in freelancing. Always strive to deliver high-quality work by deadlines to earn positive reviews and build a strong client base.
- *Set Realistic Rates*: Starting with competitive rates can help you attract clients as you build experience. As your skills and portfolio grow, adjust your rates to reflect your value.
- *Communicate Clearly with Clients*: Good communication helps avoid misunderstandings and ensures that you and your clients are aligned on project goals and timelines.

Freelancing can be an effective way to earn extra income while doing work you enjoy. Whether it's a side hustle or the start of a new career path, freelancing allows you to utilize your skills, grow professionally, and create an additional income stream tailored to your schedule and goals.

2. Tutoring Or Coaching: Sharing Your Knowledge For Profit

If you have in-depth knowledge or expertise in a particular area, tutoring or coaching can be a rewarding way to earn additional income. Whether it's academic subjects, specialized skills like coding or music, or fields like fitness, the demand for personalized learning and coaching is steadily increasing. Platforms such as Wyzant, or even social media, can help you connect with clients eager to learn from you.

Why Consider Tutoring or Coaching?

- *Flexible Hours and Personalized Interaction*: Tutoring and coaching provide the flexibility to schedule sessions that fit your availability, while allowing for meaningful, one-on-one interactions with clients.
- *High Demand Across Various Fields*: There's a consistent need for tutors in academic subjects, especially STEM and language courses, while coaches are in demand for career, wellness, and business guidance.
- *Opportunity to Make a Positive Impact*: Helping others learn or improve a skill can be highly rewarding, as you're contributing to their growth and development.

Getting Started with Tutoring or Coaching

- *Define Your Niche*: Consider your areas of expertise and the type of clients you want to serve. For tutoring, you might specialize in math, languages, or standardized test preparation. For coaching, you could focus on areas like career development, fitness, business strategy, or personal wellness.
- *Create a Profile on Tutoring Platforms*: Platforms like Wyzant, Preply, or Varsity Tutors allow you to create a professional profile and connect with students seeking help in your area of expertise.

- *Leverage Social Media or Build a Website*: Promote your services on social media or create a personal website to reach a broader audience. Highlight your qualifications, experience, and any client testimonials to build credibility.
- *Offer Introductory Sessions*: Consider offering an introductory session at a reduced rate to attract new clients. This allows potential clients to experience your teaching style before committing to ongoing sessions.

Tips for Success

- *Prepare Personalized Lesson Plans*: Tailor each session to meet the unique needs of your clients. For example, in tutoring, customize your teaching based on the student's learning style and goals. In coaching, align your guidance with the client's specific objectives and challenges.
- *Set Competitive Rates*: Research the going rates for tutors or coaches in your field to ensure your pricing is competitive. As you gain experience and positive reviews, adjust your rates accordingly.
- *Build Strong Client Relationships*: Effective communication and a genuine investment in your client's progress foster trust and satisfaction, increasing the likelihood of repeat sessions and referrals.

Tutoring and coaching offer an avenue to share your knowledge while generating income. Whether you're helping students excel in school, guiding individuals toward career advancement, or supporting others in their wellness journeys, tutoring and coaching allow you to make a positive impact and leverage your expertise.

3. Selling Products Online: Turning Hobbies Or

Retail Skills Into Profit

Selling products online is an excellent way to transform your creative skills or business ideas into a source of income. Whether you're handcrafting unique items, designing clothing, creating artwork, or want to launch a product-based business, online platforms make it accessible. For those without a physical product or who want to avoid inventory costs, dropshipping offers a low-risk way to run an e-commerce business.

Why Sell Products Online?

- *Flexible and Scalable*: Selling online allows you to reach a global audience and scale your business over time, working on your own schedule.
- *Diverse Options*: From handmade goods to dropshipping, the online market offers multiple ways to tailor your business to your skills, interests, and resources.
- *Potential for Passive Income*: With dropshipping or digital products, you can create systems that generate revenue with minimal ongoing effort.

Getting Started with Selling Products Online

- *Decide What to Sell*: If you create your own products, focus on items that showcase your craftsmanship or creativity, such as jewelry, home decor, or art prints. For dropshipping, research trending products or niches that have consistent demand but relatively low competition.
- *Choose a Platform*: Popular platforms like Etsy are ideal for handmade or unique goods, while eBay can be used for a wide range of products, including vintage items. Shopify offers more control over branding for building your own online store, and it works well with dropshipping apps like Oberlo or Spocket.
- *Set Up Your Store*: Take time to create a professional,

appealing online store. Use high-quality photos, write detailed product descriptions, and price items competitively. Consider adding a personal touch by sharing the story behind your products or your brand.

Tips for Success

- *Focus on Quality and Presentation*: Quality and presentation are everything in e-commerce. For handmade products, invest in quality materials, and for dropshipping, carefully select reliable suppliers to ensure customer satisfaction. Professional product photos and engaging descriptions are essential to attract buyers.
- *Use Social Media and Marketing Tools*: Social media platforms like Instagram and Pinterest are excellent for showcasing products and connecting with potential customers. For dropshipping and e-commerce sites, consider running ads or using email marketing to reach more buyers.
- *Provide Excellent Customer Service*: Build trust and encourage repeat business by responding promptly to customer inquiries, handling issues professionally, and ensuring orders are processed on time. Positive reviews and satisfied customers can help grow your business through word-of-mouth and increased visibility on e-commerce platforms.

Selling products online offers a variety of avenues for creative expression and business innovation. Whether you're selling handmade crafts or launching a dropshipping store, the potential to reach a wide audience and generate income is substantial. With the right approach, selling online can become a rewarding and sustainable source of income that leverages your skills and passions.

4. Delivery Or Rideshare Services: Earn While On The Move

Driving for rideshare companies like Uber or Lyft, or delivering food through services like DoorDash, Instacart, or Uber Eats, can be a convenient and flexible way to earn extra income. This type of work is appealing because it allows you to set your own hours and work as much or as little as you like, fitting around other commitments.

Why Consider Delivery or Rideshare Services?

- *Flexible Hours*: You have complete control over when and how often you work, making it easy to earn money around other jobs or responsibilities.
- *Immediate Earnings*: These platforms often pay weekly, and some even offer options to cash out earnings instantly, which can be helpful if you need quick cash.
- *Minimal Qualifications*: Requirements are typically straightforward—usually just a valid driver's license, a suitable vehicle, and a background check.

Getting Started with Delivery or Rideshare Services

- *Choose the Right Platform*: Decide which type of service aligns with your interests and vehicle. Rideshare driving with Uber or Lyft is great if you prefer interacting with passengers, while food delivery with DoorDash, Instacart, or Uber Eats lets you work solo.
- *Meet Vehicle and Background Requirements*: Most platforms have specific vehicle requirements, such as a certain model year, number of doors, and insurance standards. Background checks are typically required as well.

- *Download the App and Start*: Once approved, you'll use the platform's app to receive orders or ride requests. Apps show you where to pick up and drop off, making it easy to navigate each trip.

Tips for Success

- *Plan for High-Demand Times*: Peak hours (like evenings and weekends for rideshares, and lunch or dinner for food delivery) usually come with more requests and may offer higher pay rates or bonuses. Working during these times can boost your earnings.
- *Keep an Eye on Incentives and Bonuses*: Many platforms offer incentives, such as bonuses for completing a certain number of trips within a timeframe. Take advantage of these opportunities when they align with your schedule.
- *Maintain a Good Rating*: Providing excellent customer service and ensuring timely deliveries help you maintain a high rating, which can lead to better opportunities and tips.
- *Factor in Costs*: Remember to consider vehicle-related expenses like gas, maintenance, and insurance. Tracking these costs can give you a clearer view of your actual earnings and help you maximize profits.

Driving for rideshare or delivery services can be an effective way to generate income on your own schedule. Whether it's a part-time gig or a way to supplement your earnings, these platforms offer a flexible approach to earning money with minimal setup, making them a popular option for those looking for additional income streams.

Step 3: Explore Passive Income Opportunities

Passive income refers to money that you earn with little ongoing effort, once the initial work is done. While building passive income streams often requires upfront investment of time or money, the goal is to create revenue sources that generate income consistently without much hands-on work.

Here are a few passive income ideas:

1. Invest In Dividend-Paying Stocks: Building A Stream Of Passive Income

Dividend-paying stocks are an attractive option for those looking to earn passive income while potentially growing their wealth. These stocks represent shares of companies that distribute a portion of their profits back to shareholders regularly in the form of dividends. By investing in these stocks, you can receive consistent income, regardless of whether the stock price fluctuates.

Why Invest in Dividend-Paying Stocks?

- *Steady Income Stream*: Dividend stocks offer a regular payout, usually quarterly, making them a reliable income source. This can be particularly useful during retirement or for building wealth over time.
- *Compounding Power through Reinvestment*: By reinvesting dividends, you can purchase additional shares and compound your returns over the long term. Many brokerages offer automatic dividend reinvestment plans (DRIPs), allowing your portfolio to grow steadily.
- *Potential for Growth and Stability*: Many dividend-paying companies are well-established, financially stable businesses. Dividend stocks can offer growth potential, making them suitable for long-term investors who want both income and stability.

Getting Started with Dividend Investing

- *Research Dividend Stocks*: Look for companies with a strong history of paying and growing dividends, often known as "Dividend Aristocrats" or "Dividend Kings." These are companies that have increased their dividends for 25+ consecutive years, which can be a sign of stability.
- *Choose a Dividend Yield That Matches Your Goals*: Dividend yield is the percentage of a stock's price that a company pays out in dividends annually. A high yield can be appealing, but it's essential to assess the company's overall health to ensure the dividend is sustainable.
- *Consider a Dividend-Focused ETF or Mutual Fund*: If you're new to investing or prefer a diversified approach, dividend-focused exchange-traded funds (ETFs) or mutual funds can provide exposure to a variety of dividend-paying companies, spreading risk and simplifying portfolio management.

Tips for Success

- *Focus on Quality, Not Just Yield*: While high-yield stocks can be tempting, prioritize financially strong companies with consistent dividend growth. Extremely high yields can sometimes be unsustainable or indicate underlying business issues.
- *Diversify Your Portfolio*: Don't rely solely on one or two dividend stocks. Aim to diversify across sectors and industries to reduce risk and create a more balanced portfolio.
- *Keep an Eye on Fees*: Some brokers charge fees for buying and reinvesting dividends. Look for low-cost or fee-free options to maximize your earnings over time.
- *Be Patient*: Dividend investing is a long-term strategy. By reinvesting dividends and allowing your portfolio to grow, you can benefit from compounding returns, leading to substantial income in the future.

Dividend-paying stocks offer a straightforward approach to building passive income while providing the potential for long-term growth. By focusing on high-quality companies and reinvesting dividends, you can create a source of income that grows over time, supporting your financial goals.

2. Create An Online Course Or Digital Product: Monetize Your Knowledge

If you have valuable knowledge or a specialized skill, creating an online course, e-book, or other digital product can be a lucrative way to generate passive income. After the initial effort of creating and marketing your product, it can continue to sell, providing ongoing earnings. Platforms like Teachable, Udemy, and Gumroad make it straightforward to design, host, and sell digital products to a global audience.

Why Create an Online Course or Digital Product?

- *Potential for Passive Income*: Once your product is created, it can sell repeatedly without requiring much additional effort, making it an ideal source of passive income.
- *Scalable Earnings*: There's no limit to the number of people who can buy your digital product, allowing your income to scale as your audience grows.
- *Flexible and Low-Cost*: With minimal overhead and production costs, digital products are cost-effective, especially when compared to physical goods.

Getting Started with Your Digital Product

- *Identify Your Niche*: Think about areas where you have expertise and that others are eager to learn about. Skills like coding, graphic design, personal finance, or cooking

often attract large audiences.
- *Choose a Platform*: Platforms like Teachable, Udemy, and Skillshare are well-suited for hosting courses, while Gumroad and Amazon Kindle Direct Publishing work well for e-books and other downloadable products.
- *Create Valuable Content*: Design your course or product to be comprehensive and engaging. Whether it's videos, written content, or interactive assignments, high-quality content is essential for building a product that people will find worthwhile.

Tips for Success

- *Plan Your Content Carefully*: Organize your material in a way that makes it easy for your audience to follow. For a course, create modules that progress logically and cover essential aspects of the topic.
- *Invest in Presentation*: High-quality visuals and sound can make a big difference. Consider a good microphone and camera if you're creating a video course, and pay attention to layout and design if you're creating an e-book or PDF guide.
- *Promote Your Product Effectively*: While platforms like Udemy may help with promotion, it's essential to leverage social media, blogs, and email marketing to reach a wider audience.
- *Consider Feedback and Improvement*: Feedback is invaluable for refining your product. Use reviews or ask customers directly for feedback to improve your content, keeping it relevant and valuable over time.

Creating an online course or digital product is a powerful way to share your knowledge, build a brand, and create a lasting income stream. By focusing on quality and marketing, you can build a product that reaches people worldwide and continues to generate revenue long after its launch.

3. Rental Income: Building Wealth Through Real Estate

If you have the resources to invest in real estate, owning rental property can be a lucrative way to earn passive income. Investing in rental properties can be a rewarding way to generate passive income and build long-term wealth. Whether you choose traditional long-term rentals or short-term rentals through platforms like Airbnb, rental properties can create a steady income stream. However, managing a rental property does involve some active work, from finding tenants to handling maintenance and repairs.

Why Consider Rental Income?

- *Regular Cash Flow*: Rental properties provide consistent income that can help cover your mortgage and other expenses, with the potential for profit if rental income exceeds these costs.
- *Appreciation Potential*: Real estate often appreciates over time, adding value to your investment as the property's market price increases.
- *Tax Benefits*: Rental property owners can deduct expenses like mortgage interest, property taxes, and maintenance costs. Additionally, depreciation can provide a tax shield, reducing taxable income.

Types of Rental Properties

- *Long-Term Rentals*: Leasing to tenants on a yearly basis provides reliable income and requires less frequent tenant turnover.
- *Short-Term Rentals*: Platforms like Airbnb make it easy to rent out properties on a nightly or weekly basis. This

can be more profitable but also demands more active management and may have additional regulations.

Getting Started with Rental Income

- *Assess Your Finances and Investment Goals*: Rental properties often require a significant upfront investment, including a down payment, closing costs, and possibly renovation expenses. Ensure you have a clear budget and plan for funding.
- *Choose the Right Property*: Location is crucial for rental properties. Look for areas with strong rental demand, nearby amenities, and future growth potential.
- *Research Local Laws and Regulations*: Rental property laws vary by region, especially for short-term rentals, which are often subject to stricter regulations. Be sure to comply with zoning, licensing, and tax requirements.

Tips for Success

- *Screen Tenants Carefully*: For long-term rentals, conduct thorough tenant screenings to ensure reliable rent payments and minimize turnover. This step can reduce risks and keep your property in good condition.
- *Consider Property Management*: If you'd prefer not to manage day-to-day tasks, hiring a property management company can simplify things. They handle tenant interactions, repairs, and other management responsibilities for a fee, typically around 8-12% of monthly rent.
- *Budget for Maintenance and Repairs*: Maintenance is essential to keep your property attractive and functional. Set aside a portion of rental income to cover repairs, updates, and unexpected costs.
- *Monitor Market Trends*: Keep an eye on rental market trends and local economic changes that could impact rental demand or pricing. Adjust your pricing and

strategy as needed to maintain profitability.

Rental properties can be a powerful tool for generating income and building wealth. By investing in the right property and maintaining it well, rental income can become a sustainable source of financial stability. With a solid plan and careful management, rental properties have the potential to provide both immediate cash flow and long-term investment gains.

4. Peer-To-Peer Lending: Earn Passive Income By Lending To Borrowers

Peer-to-peer (P2P) lending platforms like LendingClub and Prosper enable you to lend money directly to individuals or small businesses in exchange for interest payments. This can be a convenient way to earn passive income as borrowers repay their loans with interest. P2P lending offers potentially higher returns than traditional savings accounts or bonds, but it does come with risks, as there is always a chance borrowers may default.

Why Consider Peer-to-Peer Lending?

- *Higher Potential Returns*: P2P lending can offer higher returns compared to savings accounts or other conservative investments, often with interest rates ranging from 5% to 15% depending on the risk profile.
- *Flexibility and Control*: P2P platforms allow you to choose specific loans based on risk levels, loan terms, and borrower profiles, enabling you to manage your investment according to your risk tolerance.
- *Diversification Opportunity*: P2P lending provides a way to diversify your investment portfolio with a different asset class that's not directly tied to stock market performance.

Getting Started with Peer-to-Peer Lending

- *Choose a Reputable Platform*: Research platforms like LendingClub, Prosper, or others available in your country. Each platform has different requirements, fees, and interest rates, so choose one that aligns with your financial goals.
- *Set an Investment Budget*: Determine how much you're willing to invest and what percentage of your portfolio you'd like to allocate to P2P lending. It's wise to start with a conservative amount, especially if you're new to this type of investment.
- *Select Loans Based on Risk Level*: Most platforms categorize loans by risk level. High-risk loans offer higher interest rates but come with a greater chance of default, while low-risk loans offer lower returns with a higher likelihood of repayment.

Tips for Success

- *Diversify Across Multiple Loans*: Instead of investing a large sum in a single loan, spread your investment across multiple loans to minimize risk. Many platforms allow you to invest as little as $25 per loan, making it easier to diversify.
- *Reinvest Your Earnings*: Reinvesting the principal and interest payments you receive can compound your returns over time, leading to greater passive income.
- *Monitor Default Rates*: Keep an eye on the default rates for your chosen risk level. Some platforms provide analytics to help you track performance and adjust your investment strategy as needed.
- *Be Prepared for Potential Losses*: P2P lending is not risk-free. Borrowers may default, leading to potential losses. Consider setting aside a portion of your earnings as a buffer to offset any losses that occur.

P2P lending can be a worthwhile way to generate passive income, especially if you're looking for an alternative investment that's relatively uncorrelated with the stock market. While it's important to be aware of the risks, careful loan selection and diversification can help manage those risks and optimize your returns. By balancing risk and reward, P2P lending can become a valuable part of a well-rounded investment strategy.

5. Affiliate Marketing: Earn Commissions By Recommending Products You Trust

Affiliate marketing allows you to earn passive income by promoting products or services online. When someone makes a purchase through your referral link, you earn a commission. This is a versatile income stream, especially if you have a blog, social media following, or YouTube channel. By recommending products or services that align with your audience's interests, you can build credibility and generate income simultaneously. Popular programs include Amazon's Affiliate Program and affiliate networks like ShareASale and Commission Junction (CJ).

Why Consider Affiliate Marketing?

- *Low Startup Costs*: Affiliate marketing requires minimal initial investment. You don't need to create a product or handle customer service; you simply refer customers to products you endorse.
- *Passive Income Potential*: Once you've created content with affiliate links, it can continue to generate income as people discover and click on your links over time.
- *Flexibility in Niches*: Affiliate programs exist for nearly every industry, from tech gadgets to fashion to fitness, so you can choose products that resonate with your audience.

Getting Started with Affiliate Marketing

- *Identify Your Niche and Audience*: Choose products or services that align with your content's theme and audience. For example, if you have a travel blog, look for affiliate programs related to travel gear, accommodation, or travel insurance.
- *Sign Up for Affiliate Programs*: Join affiliate programs directly through companies or via affiliate networks like Amazon Associates, ShareASale, or CJ. Look for programs with competitive commission rates and strong product offerings.
- *Create Quality Content*: Incorporate affiliate links naturally within valuable content, such as product reviews, tutorials, or recommendation lists. Content that provides genuine value is more likely to gain trust and encourage clicks.

Tips for Success

- *Be Transparent*: Always disclose affiliate relationships to maintain transparency and trust with your audience. Most countries have legal requirements for affiliate disclosure, so check the guidelines in your region.
- *Focus on Products You Believe In*: Recommending products you genuinely like and use enhances credibility. Your audience is more likely to make purchases if they sense your authentic endorsement.
- *Optimize SEO for Discoverability*: SEO (search engine optimization) can increase the visibility of your content, making it easier for potential customers to find your affiliate links. Research relevant keywords and incorporate them naturally.
- *Track Performance and Adjust*: Use tracking tools provided by affiliate programs to see which links and products are performing best. Adjust your strategy

based on what resonates most with your audience.

Affiliate marketing can be a profitable source of passive income when done thoughtfully and strategically. By focusing on content that serves your audience and promoting products that add real value, you can build a long-term affiliate marketing income that grows as your online presence expands.

6. Network Marketing: Building Income Through Relationships

Network marketing, also known as multi-level marketing (MLM), is a business model where individuals earn income through direct sales of products and by recruiting others into the business. In network marketing, you can create a passive income stream by building a team of distributors who also sell products and recruit new members. This model emphasizes relationship-building and can be lucrative for those who excel in sales and networking.

Why Consider Network Marketing?

- *Low Startup Costs*: Many network marketing companies have low entry fees, allowing you to start your own business without significant investment. You often only need to purchase a starter kit to get going.
- *Flexibility*: Network marketing offers the flexibility to work on your own schedule, making it an attractive option for those seeking additional income alongside a full-time job or other commitments.
- *Potential for Passive Income*: As you build your network and train new distributors, you can earn commissions from their sales, creating a potential passive income stream as your team grows.

Getting Started with Network Marketing

- *Choose the Right Company*: Research various network marketing companies and their product offerings. Consider factors such as the company's reputation, product demand, compensation plan, and the support they provide to distributors.
- *Understand the Compensation Plan*: Familiarize yourself with how commissions and bonuses are structured. Some companies offer tiered commissions, while others provide bonuses for recruiting new members or achieving sales targets.
- *Build Your Network*: Start building your customer base and team. This involves reaching out to friends, family, and acquaintances, as well as leveraging social media and other platforms to expand your reach.

Tips for Success

- *Focus on Product Knowledge*: Understanding the products you're selling is crucial. Being knowledgeable allows you to effectively communicate benefits and answer customer questions, which can help increase sales.
- *Emphasize Relationship Building*: Network marketing relies heavily on personal relationships. Building trust and maintaining good communication with your customers and team members can lead to sustained success.
- *Provide Support and Training*: If you recruit others, offer them guidance and support. Successful teams thrive on mentorship and shared success, which can help grow your network more effectively.
- *Be Ethical and Transparent*: Avoid aggressive sales tactics that can damage relationships. Focus on providing genuine value and ensuring that your offerings are suitable for your audience.

Caution

While network marketing offers opportunities for income, it's important to be aware of the risks. Success often requires significant time, effort, and skill in sales and recruiting. Some network marketing companies can have high turnover rates and may not be as financially rewarding as they claim. Researching thoroughly and understanding the business model is crucial before committing.

Network marketing can be a viable way to generate income, especially if you excel in networking and relationship-building. By focusing on providing value, training your team, and maintaining ethical practices, you can build a successful network marketing business that offers both active and passive income opportunities.

Step 4: Start A Small Business

If you're ready to commit more time and effort, starting a small business can provide a substantial source of additional income and even grow into your main income stream over time. While starting a business requires careful planning, dedication, and often some upfront capital, it can also lead to significant financial rewards and personal fulfillment.

Here are a few small business ideas to consider:

1. Service-Based Business: Turning Skills Into Income

Starting a service-based business can be a fulfilling and profitable venture. By leveraging your skills, knowledge, and expertise, you can provide valuable services to individuals or businesses while earning an income. Service-based businesses cover a wide range of industries, including landscaping, cleaning, consulting, photography, and more.

Why Consider a Service-Based Business?

- *Low Startup Costs*: Many service-based businesses require minimal upfront investment, often just the tools or equipment needed to deliver your service. This makes it accessible for many entrepreneurs.
- *High Demand*: There's often a consistent demand for various services, as individuals and businesses are willing to pay for expertise and convenience. This can lead to a steady stream of clients if you market effectively.
- *Flexibility*: Service-based businesses can offer flexibility in terms of hours and location, allowing you to set your own schedule and potentially work from home or remotely.

Getting Started with a Service-Based Business

- *Identify Your Niche*: Determine which services you can provide based on your skills and market demand. Consider what you enjoy doing and where you can offer the most value.
- *Create a Business Plan*: Outline your business goals, target market, pricing structure, and marketing strategies. A solid plan will guide you as you start and grow your business.
- *Market Your Services*: Utilize various marketing strategies to attract clients. This can include creating a website, leveraging social media, networking in your community, and asking for referrals from satisfied clients.

Tips for Success

- *Build a Strong Brand*: Establishing a recognizable

brand can set you apart from competitors. Create a professional logo, develop a unique value proposition, and ensure consistent messaging across all platforms.
- *Focus on Customer Service*: Providing exceptional customer service can lead to repeat business and referrals. Listen to your clients, be responsive, and exceed their expectations to build strong relationships.
- *Network and Collaborate*: Attend local events, join professional organizations, and collaborate with other businesses to expand your reach and build connections within your industry.
- *Invest in Continuous Learning*: Stay updated with industry trends and continuously improve your skills. Consider taking courses or attending workshops to enhance your expertise and service offerings.

Common Types of Service-Based Businesses

- **Landscaping and Gardening**: Offering lawn care, garden design, and maintenance services.
- **Cleaning Services**: Providing residential or commercial cleaning, organizing, or specialty cleaning services.
- **Consulting**: Leveraging your professional experience to advise businesses or individuals in areas like marketing, finance, or operations.
- **Photography and Videography**: Capturing events, portraits, or commercial work for clients.

Service-based businesses can be a rewarding way to earn income while helping others. By identifying your strengths, effectively marketing your services, and providing exceptional customer experiences, you can build a successful service-based business that meets both your financial and personal goals.

2. E-Commerce Business: Capitalizing On The Online Shopping Boom

Starting an e-commerce business offers a fantastic opportunity to tap into the growing trend of online shopping. With the convenience of the internet, you can reach customers around the globe and sell products in a variety of ways, whether they are your own creations, sourced from wholesalers, or dropshipped directly to customers.

Why Consider an E-Commerce Business?

- **Global Reach**: Unlike traditional brick-and-mortar stores, an e-commerce business allows you to reach a worldwide audience, significantly expanding your potential customer base.
- **Flexibility**: You can operate your e-commerce business from anywhere, giving you the flexibility to set your own hours and work from any location.
- **Lower Overhead Costs**: Many e-commerce models, especially dropshipping, require less upfront investment in inventory and physical storefronts, leading to lower operating costs.

Getting Started with an E-Commerce Business

1. **Choose Your Niche**: Identify a specific market or product category that interests you and has demand. Consider trends, target demographics, and what sets your offerings apart from competitors.
2. **Select a Business Model**:
    a. **Direct Sales**: Selling products you create or purchase wholesale to resell.
    b. **Dropshipping**: Partnering with suppliers who handle inventory and shipping, allowing you to sell without holding stock.
    c. **Print on Demand**: Creating custom products (like apparel or home decor) that are printed and shipped by a third-party supplier only

when an order is made.
3. **Set Up Your Online Store**: Choose an e-commerce platform such as Shopify, WooCommerce, or BigCommerce to build your online store. Customize your site with product descriptions, images, and a user-friendly layout.
4. **Payment Processing**: Set up secure payment processing options to accept payments from customers easily. Services like PayPal, Stripe, or Square are popular choices.

Tips for Success

- **Optimize for SEO**: Implement search engine optimization (SEO) strategies to improve your online visibility and attract organic traffic. Research relevant keywords and use them in your product descriptions and blog content.
- **Market Your Store**: Use digital marketing strategies, including social media advertising, email marketing, and content marketing, to drive traffic to your e-commerce site. Collaborate with influencers or run promotions to boost awareness.
- **Focus on Customer Experience**: Provide excellent customer service and user experience. Ensure your website is easy to navigate, offer clear return policies, and respond promptly to customer inquiries.
- **Analyze and Adapt**: Use analytics tools to track sales, customer behavior, and website traffic. Regularly analyze your performance data to understand what's working and where adjustments are needed to improve sales.

Common Types of E-Commerce Businesses

- **Retail E-Commerce**: Selling physical products directly to consumers, such as clothing, electronics, or home goods.

- **Digital Products**: Selling downloadable products like e-books, software, or online courses.
- **Subscription Boxes**: Offering curated boxes of products delivered to customers regularly, focusing on niche markets like beauty, snacks, or fitness.
- **Marketplace Selling**: Selling on established platforms like Amazon, eBay, or Etsy to leverage their audience while managing your own storefront.

An e-commerce business can provide significant income potential and scalability. By choosing the right niche, optimizing your store, and implementing effective marketing strategies, you can establish a successful online business that capitalizes on the ever-growing demand for online shopping.

3. Subscription-Based Business: Building A Steady Stream Of Recurring Income

A subscription-based business model offers a compelling way to generate consistent, recurring revenue. By providing customers with regular access to products or services for a monthly fee, you can create a reliable income stream while fostering customer loyalty and engagement. This model is popular across various industries, from physical products to digital content.

Why Consider a Subscription-Based Business?

- **Predictable Revenue**: Subscriptions provide a stable income flow, allowing for better financial planning and cash flow management.
- **Customer Loyalty**: Subscriptions often foster a sense of commitment among customers, leading to long-term relationships and higher retention rates.
- **Scalability**: As your subscriber base grows, you can scale your offerings and streamline operations to accommodate more customers without significantly

increasing costs.

Getting Started with a Subscription-Based Business

1. **Identify Your Niche**: Choose a market that interests you and has demand for subscription services. Popular niches include beauty, food, fitness, and digital content.
2. **Define Your Offerings**: Determine what you will provide to your subscribers. This could be curated product boxes, access to exclusive content, or memberships that include special perks.
3. **Choose a Pricing Model**: Set a pricing strategy that reflects the value of your offering while remaining competitive. Consider options like monthly, quarterly, or annual subscriptions.
4. **Build an Online Platform**: Create a user-friendly website or utilize subscription management platforms (such as Cratejoy or Subbly) to manage subscriptions, payments, and customer accounts.

Tips for Success

- **Deliver Value**: Ensure that your products or services provide real value to subscribers. This might include high-quality items, exclusive access, or personalized experiences that exceed their expectations.
- **Market Effectively**: Utilize digital marketing strategies to attract subscribers. Leverage social media, email marketing, and influencer partnerships to reach your target audience and promote your subscription offerings.
- **Engage and Retain Customers**: Maintain engagement with your subscribers through regular communication, personalized recommendations, and exclusive perks. Consider surveys or feedback loops to understand customer preferences better.
- **Analyze and Adapt**: Regularly evaluate subscriber feedback and business performance metrics. Use this

data to refine your offerings, improve customer satisfaction, and adjust your marketing strategies as needed.

Common Types of Subscription-Based Businesses

- **Subscription Boxes**: Monthly deliveries of curated products based on themes, such as beauty products, snacks, or fitness gear.
- **Membership Programs**: Access to exclusive content, services, or products, often in areas like fitness, education, or entertainment.
- **Digital Subscriptions**: Subscription access to software, online courses, or streaming services for movies, music, or gaming.
- **Content Subscriptions**: Memberships for premium content such as newsletters, podcasts, or exclusive articles.

A subscription-based business can provide a reliable source of income and foster lasting customer relationships. By focusing on delivering value and maintaining customer engagement, you can build a successful subscription model that grows and adapts with your audience's needs.

Step 5: Stay Organized And Manage Your Time

Building multiple streams of income requires good time management and organization. It's important to balance your main job with your side hustles, ensuring that you don't overextend yourself or burn out. Use tools like calendars, project management apps, and time trackers to stay organized and manage your income streams effectively.

Additionally, consider automating as many processes as possible. For example, if you're selling products online, you can automate inventory management, customer communication, and payment processing. If you're investing, you can set up automatic contributions to your investment accounts to ensure consistent growth.

Step 6: Protect Your Income Streams

As you diversify your income, it's essential to protect what you've built. Consider setting aside a portion of your extra earnings into an emergency fund, so you're prepared for unexpected expenses or economic downturns. Additionally, investing in insurance (such as liability insurance for a business or rental property) can safeguard your income streams from unforeseen risks.

Finally, as your side hustles and businesses grow, you may want to consult a tax professional to ensure that you're managing your income efficiently and taking advantage of any tax benefits available to entrepreneurs or investors.

Conclusion: Take Control Of Your Financial Future

Building multiple streams of income is one of the most powerful strategies for achieving financial independence. By diversifying your earnings through side hustles, passive income, and investments, you create more opportunities for financial growth and security. Whether you start small with a freelance gig or take the leap into a full-scale business, the key is to take action and stay consistent.

In the next chapter, we'll discuss how to protect and preserve your growing wealth through smart financial strategies, ensuring that you can enjoy the fruits of your labor for years to come.

CHAPTER 7: MASTERING THE THOUSANDAIRE MINDSET

Creating lasting financial success isn't just about strategies and tactics; it's about adopting the right mindset. Your mindset shapes how you approach money, influences your decisions, and ultimately determines your financial outcomes. A "thousandaire mindset" is focused on long-term growth, delayed gratification, and making deliberate, thoughtful choices. In this chapter, we'll discuss the mental barriers that often prevent people from saving and investing, such as fear, instant gratification, and lack of confidence. You'll also learn how to develop habits that align with your financial goals.

Why Mindset Matters

Your financial mindset is the set of beliefs, attitudes, and perceptions you hold about money. It affects how you spend, save, and invest and influences the types of goals you set for yourself. Even with the best financial plan, an unhelpful mindset can sabotage your progress. Developing a mindset of discipline, resilience, and patience can help you not only achieve financial milestones but also sustain them in the long term.

With a strong thousandaire mindset, you'll be better equipped to:

- Resist temptations for instant gratification.
- Make thoughtful spending and investment decisions.
- Stay committed to your financial goals, even when challenges arise.
- Think strategically and stay focused on long-term success.

Step 1: Understand And Overcome Mental Barriers

To master a positive financial mindset, you need to recognize and address the common mental barriers that may be holding you back. Here are a few of the most prevalent:

1. Fear of Financial Risks

For many people, the idea of investing or making big financial decisions triggers fear. This fear often stems from a lack of knowledge or a fear of losing money. However, not taking any risks can limit your financial growth.

Solution: Educate yourself on financial topics and start small. By building your knowledge, you'll gain confidence and feel more in control. Taking calculated risks—such as investing a small amount in stocks or real estate—can gradually help you overcome fear.

2. Instant Gratification

In a world of on-demand convenience, the desire for instant rewards can make it hard to save and invest for the future. Whether it's buying the latest gadget or splurging on experiences, instant gratification can derail long-term financial goals.

Solution: Shift your focus from short-term desires to long-term gains. Each time you feel the urge to spend impulsively, pause and remind yourself of your financial goals. By visualizing the future benefits of saving and investing, you'll find it easier to resist temptations.

3. Lack of Confidence

Many people feel that financial success is beyond their reach or that they lack the skills to manage money effectively. This lack of confidence can keep them from taking charge of their finances.

Solution: Start by setting small, achievable financial goals. Accomplishing these goals can build your confidence and motivate you to aim higher. Remember, financial independence is a journey, and every step forward is progress.

Step 2: Cultivate Habits Aligned With Your Financial Goals

Habits are powerful because they shape our daily lives and decisions. By developing habits that align with your financial goals, you can stay consistent and focused without feeling like you're constantly making sacrifices.

1. Track Your Finances Regularly

Develop the habit of checking in on your finances at least once a week. Review your budget, track your spending, and look at your savings and investments. This practice keeps you informed and in control, helping you identify any areas where you might be veering off course.

2. Practice Delayed Gratification

Train yourself to wait before making non-essential purchases. For example, adopt a 24-hour rule for any purchase over a certain amount. By waiting, you give yourself time to evaluate whether the expense aligns with your goals or if it's just a fleeting desire.

3. Pay Yourself First

Set up automatic transfers from your checking account to your savings or investment account each payday. This ensures that you're saving consistently before spending on other expenses. By "paying yourself first," you'll build your savings automatically and prioritize your financial goals.

4. Invest in Self-Education

The more you understand about personal finance, investing, and wealth-building strategies, the better equipped you'll be to make smart financial decisions. Make a habit of reading books, listening to podcasts, or attending workshops on financial topics. This ongoing education will empower you and help you keep a growth-oriented mindset.

Step 3: Set Clear, Achievable Financial Goals

A key component of the thousandaire mindset is setting

realistic goals. Clear goals provide direction and motivation, making it easier to resist short-term temptations and stay focused. Here's how to set effective financial goals:

1. Start with Small, Actionable Goals

Break down your larger financial goals into smaller, manageable steps. For example, if your goal is to save $1,000, set a mini-goal of saving $100 each month. These small wins build momentum and keep you motivated.

2. Use the SMART Framework

SMART goals are Specific, Measurable, Achievable, Relevant, and Time-bound. Instead of setting a vague goal like "save more money," try "save $500 in three months by reducing dining out and entertainment expenses." A SMART goal is easier to track and accomplish.

3. Celebrate Progress Along the Way

Celebrate your financial wins, no matter how small. Recognizing your progress helps reinforce the positive habits you're building and keeps you motivated to continue. Each milestone achieved is a step closer to your ultimate financial goals.

Step 4: Adopt A Growth Mindset

A growth mindset, as opposed to a fixed mindset, embraces the idea that skills, knowledge, and even wealth can be developed over time. People with a growth mindset view challenges as opportunities to learn and grow. By adopting a growth mindset, you'll see setbacks as temporary and be more resilient in the face of financial obstacles.

1. Embrace Mistakes as Learning Opportunities

Instead of being discouraged by mistakes or failures, use them as learning opportunities. Whether it's a poor investment choice or an unplanned expense, analyze what happened and what you can learn from it. Mistakes are part of the journey, and learning from them will make you a stronger, smarter investor.

2. Surround Yourself with Supportive Influences

Your environment influences your mindset and behaviors, so surround yourself with people who share similar financial values and goals. Seek out mentors, join online communities focused on financial independence, and limit exposure to negative influences that encourage reckless spending or discourage savings.

3. Visualize Your Financial Future

Visualization can be a powerful motivator. Take time to envision what financial independence looks like for you. Picture yourself achieving your goals, whether it's owning a home, being debt-free, or traveling without financial worries. By regularly visualizing your success, you reinforce your motivation to stay on track.

Step 5: Develop A Positive Relationship With Money

Money is often a source of stress, fear, or guilt, but cultivating a positive relationship with it can transform the way you manage and think about your finances. Embrace money as a tool that can help you achieve your goals, rather than as a source of stress or limitation.

1. Shift Your Language About Money

Be mindful of how you talk and think about money. Replace negative thoughts like "I'll never be good with money" with empowering statements like "I'm learning to manage my money effectively." Positive self-talk reinforces confidence and a healthy financial mindset.

2. Focus on Value Over Cost

When making spending decisions, focus on value rather than just the price. Ask yourself if a purchase brings lasting value to your life or if it's simply a short-term expense. By focusing on value, you'll make smarter spending choices that align with your goals.

3. Practice Gratitude for What You Have

Gratitude helps shift your focus from what you lack to what you already have. By appreciating the resources, skills, and progress you've made, you'll be less likely to feel the need to "keep up with the Joneses" and more likely to feel satisfied with your own journey.

Conclusion: The Power Of A Thousandaire Mindset

Achieving financial success begins with the right mindset. A thousandaire mindset emphasizes discipline, patience, and resilience. By overcoming mental barriers, cultivating helpful habits, setting achievable goals, and adopting a positive relationship with money, you'll be well on your way to creating lasting financial security.

In the following chapter, we'll explore practical strategies to protect your financial progress and ensure that the wealth you're building is safeguarded against risks and unforeseen challenges.

CHAPTER 8: FINANCIAL LITERACY:

Knowledge is Power

Financial literacy is the key to long-term wealth. In this chapter, we'll explore the basics of financial education—understanding interest rates, how credit works, and the significance of financial terms like "APR," "equity," and "capital gains." This knowledge will empower you to make informed decisions and avoid costly mistakes. We'll also talk about how to continue growing your financial knowledge over time.

These fundamentals empower you to avoid costly mistakes that can derail financial progress, such as high-interest debt or unfavorable loan terms. Alongside these basics, we'll dive into strategies for continuing your financial education—whether through books, courses, or trusted online resources—to keep your knowledge growing over time and adapt to changes in the financial landscape.

Ready to build a solid financial foundation? Let's dive in!

Interest Rates – How They Work For Or Against You

Interest rates are a fundamental part of the financial world.

Whether you're borrowing money or saving it, interest plays a crucial role in determining how much you pay or earn over time. Here's how understanding interest can help you make better decisions:

1. When Interest Works for You (Saving and Investing):

When you save money in a bank account or invest, the bank or investment firm often pays you interest. This is called *compound interest*, where you earn interest on both the initial amount you deposited (principal) and on the interest that accumulates. Compound interest allows your savings to grow faster, especially over long periods. For example, a small investment earning a steady interest rate can significantly increase in value through compounding, benefiting your financial future.

2. When Interest Works Against You (Borrowing and Debt):

When you borrow money, whether through a loan, mortgage, or credit card, you're typically required to pay interest to the lender. In these cases, interest rates can work against you, especially if you have high-interest debt like credit card balances. High-interest rates make debt harder to pay off because a significant portion of your payment may go toward interest rather than reducing the principal. Understanding this can motivate you to prioritize paying off high-interest debt to save money in the long run.

3. Fixed vs. Variable Interest Rates:
   a. *Fixed Interest Rate*: The interest rate remains the same for the entire term of the loan or savings period. This provides stability and predictability, making budgeting easier.
   b. *Variable Interest Rate*: The rate can fluctuate over time, often based on market conditions. Variable rates can sometimes offer lower initial rates but also carry the risk of rising, potentially increasing

your costs over time.

4. APR (Annual Percentage Rate):

APR is the annual cost of borrowing money, including interest and any associated fees. It's a useful metric for comparing loans or credit offers, as it reflects the true cost of borrowing.

By understanding interest rates and how they impact both savings and debt, you can make informed decisions that align with your financial goals—whether it's maximizing the growth of your savings or minimizing the cost of borrowing.

Credit – How Credit Scores, Credit Limits, And Credit Cards Work

Credit plays a significant role in your financial life, influencing your ability to borrow, rent, and even get a job. Understanding how credit works—and how to manage it responsibly—can help you make the most of financial opportunities while avoiding common pitfalls. Let's break down some key components:

1. Credit Scores: The Key to Borrowing Power

- Your *credit score* is a three-digit number (typically ranging from 300 to 850) that reflects your creditworthiness. Lenders use it to gauge the risk of lending to you.
- Factors affecting your score include your payment history, total debt, length of credit history, types of credit used, and recent credit inquiries.
- A higher credit score can help you qualify for better interest rates and terms on loans, saving you money over time. Good credit can also open doors to renting homes, setting up utility accounts, and even job opportunities.

2. Credit Limits: The Maximum You Can Borrow

- Your *credit limit* is the maximum amount you can borrow on a credit card or line of credit.
- Staying well below your credit limit (known as *credit utilization*) is essential. High utilization—using more than 30% of your credit limit—can negatively impact your credit score, even if you make all payments on time.
- Regularly reviewing your credit limit and keeping your usage in check can improve your credit score and show lenders that you're a responsible borrower.

3. Credit Cards: A Tool for Building Credit and Managing Finances

- Credit cards allow you to borrow money for purchases and repay it over time. They're an easy way to build credit when used wisely.
- However, credit cards come with *APR* (Annual Percentage Rate), which determines the interest you'll pay if you carry a balance. Paying off your balance in full each month helps you avoid interest costs.
- Some credit cards offer rewards, cashback, and other perks, but it's essential to avoid overspending just to earn points. The rewards aren't worth it if they lead to high-interest debt.

4. Why Responsible Credit Management Matters

- *Timely Payments:* Paying bills on time boosts your credit score and avoids costly late fees and interest charges.
- *Avoiding Excessive Debt:* Too much debt or reliance on credit can lead to high monthly payments, stress, and limited financial flexibility.
- *Regular Credit Monitoring:* Reviewing your credit report

helps you spot errors and identity theft early, protecting your credit score.

Building a strong credit profile by managing credit responsibly opens the door to financial opportunities and helps you access credit at favorable terms when you need it. Remember, credit is a powerful tool, but only if it's used wisely!

Key Financial Terms – Understanding Apr, Equity, And Capital Gains

Familiarity with key financial terms like APR, equity, and capital gains is essential for navigating financial decisions. Let's break these down:

1. APR (Annual Percentage Rate): The True Cost of Borrowing

- *APR* represents the yearly cost of borrowing, expressed as a percentage. It includes the interest rate as well as any associated fees, making it a more accurate measure of what a loan or credit line will actually cost you over a year.
- Comparing APRs across loans, credit cards, and mortgages helps you identify the best options. A lower APR typically means a lower cost of borrowing, so understanding APR can help you save money when managing debt.

2. Equity: Your Ownership Stake

- *Equity* refers to the amount of ownership you have in an asset, often a home or a business. It's calculated as the value of the asset minus any debts owed on it. For example, if you own a home worth $300,000 and have a $200,000 mortgage, your equity in the home is

$100,000.
- Home equity can be a valuable resource; as you pay down your mortgage or as property values rise, your equity grows, which can potentially be used as collateral for loans, invested, or turned into a profit if you sell.

3. Capital Gains: Profit from Investments

- *Capital gains* refer to the profit you make when you sell an investment—like stocks, real estate, or a business asset—for more than you paid for it. For example, if you buy stock for $1,000 and sell it later for $1,500, you've made a capital gain of $500.
- There are two types of capital gains: *short-term* (for assets held less than a year) and *long-term* (for assets held over a year). Long-term capital gains are usually taxed at a lower rate, making them a more favorable option for building wealth over time.

Why Understanding These Terms Matters

Mastering these terms provides you with a framework for evaluating loans, investments, and assets. Knowing what APR means helps you avoid high-cost debt, understanding equity can guide your homeownership goals, and capital gains knowledge aids in making informed investment decisions. These insights help you move forward with confidence in your financial journey!

CHAPTER 9: HANDLING SETBACKS AND STAYING THE COURSE

No financial journey goes perfectly according to plan. Life is filled with unexpected events—medical expenses, job loss, economic downturns—that can disrupt even the best financial strategies. This chapter will guide you through strategies to prepare for and navigate these challenges without letting setbacks derail your progress toward financial stability. Here's what we'll cover:

Building An Emergency Fund: Your Financial Safety Net

As we have mentioned several times already in this book, establishing an emergency fund is a crucial step in safeguarding your financial well-being. This safety net can provide peace of mind and financial stability, allowing you to navigate unexpected expenses without derailing your budget or resorting to high-interest debt. Here's a comprehensive guide on how to get started with building your emergency savings:

1. Set a Savings Goal

- *Determine Your Target Amount*: A common recommendation is to save three to six months' worth of living expenses. This amount can vary based on individual circumstances, such as job stability, income level, and personal preferences. Consider your monthly expenses—rent or mortgage, utilities, groceries, transportation, insurance, and any other recurring costs—to calculate your target.
- *Start Small if Necessary*: If saving several months' worth of expenses feels overwhelming, start with a smaller, more manageable goal. Aim for $500 to $1,000 as an initial target, and gradually work your way up.

2. Choose the Right Savings Account

- *Select an Accessible Account*: Choose a separate savings account specifically for your emergency fund. This helps keep your emergency savings distinct from your everyday spending, reducing the temptation to dip into it for non-emergencies.
- *Look for Competitive Interest Rates*: While liquidity is crucial, consider accounts that offer competitive interest rates, such as high-yield savings accounts or money market accounts. This allows your emergency fund to grow over time while still being accessible when needed.

3. Create a Savings Plan

- *Automate Your Savings*: Set up automatic transfers from your checking account to your emergency fund. Automating savings makes it easier to prioritize this

goal and ensures that you consistently contribute, even when life gets busy.
- *Determine a Contribution Amount*: Decide how much you can reasonably contribute each month based on your budget. Even small, regular contributions add up over time, so find an amount that works for you.

4. Identify Additional Sources of Funding

- *Cut Non-Essential Expenses*: Review your monthly budget and identify areas where you can cut back temporarily to boost your savings. This might include dining out less, canceling subscriptions, or finding less expensive entertainment options.
- *Use Windfalls Wisely*: Allocate any unexpected windfalls—such as tax refunds, bonuses, or monetary gifts—directly to your emergency fund. These lump sums can significantly accelerate your savings progress.

5. Monitor and Adjust Your Fund

- *Review Regularly*: Check your emergency fund regularly to ensure it aligns with your financial goals. As your circumstances change—like an increase in living expenses or family size—reassess your savings target and adjust accordingly.
- *Celebrate Milestones*: Acknowledge your progress as you reach savings milestones. Celebrating achievements, no matter how small, can motivate you to stay committed to your goal.

6. Know When to Use Your Emergency Fund

- *Define What Constitutes an Emergency*: Clarify what types of expenses qualify as emergencies, such as unexpected medical bills, car repairs, or sudden job loss. Having clear

criteria helps you avoid misusing your fund for non-essential expenses.
- *Replenish After Use*: If you need to dip into your emergency fund, make a plan to replenish it as soon as possible. Adjust your budget or savings plan to refill the fund to maintain your financial safety net.

7. Stay Committed and Adaptable

- *Be Patient and Persistent*: Building an emergency fund takes time and discipline. Stay committed to your savings plan, and remember that progress is progress, no matter how slow.
- *Adapt to Changing Circumstances*: Life is unpredictable, and your financial situation may change. Be flexible and adjust your savings goals or contributions as necessary, ensuring that your emergency fund continues to provide the support you need.

Conclusion: The Power of Preparedness

Building an emergency fund is one of the best defenses against financial setbacks, providing you with a crucial cushion that allows you to handle unexpected expenses without falling into debt. By following these steps and maintaining a proactive approach, you'll create a financial safety net that not only protects you in times of need but also fosters peace of mind and confidence in your financial journey. Start today, and take control of your financial future!

Insurance As A Safety Net: Protecting Against Financial Setbacks

Insurance is a crucial component of financial security, serving as a safety net that helps prevent major personal crises—like illness, disability, or loss—from escalating into financial disasters. Here, we'll discuss some essential types of insurance and how to choose policies that best suit your needs.

1. Health Insurance: Covering Medical Expenses

- *Why It's Essential*: Medical emergencies and ongoing healthcare costs can be financially devastating without adequate health coverage. Health insurance helps offset the high cost of doctor visits, hospital stays, medications, and surgeries.
- *Choosing a Policy*: Look for a policy that balances your budget with the coverage you need. Consider factors like monthly premiums, deductibles (the amount you pay before insurance covers costs), and co-pays (the out-of-pocket fees you pay per service). If you have specific healthcare needs, ensure your plan covers them, as well as any regular prescriptions.

2. Disability Insurance: Replacing Income in Case of Illness or Injury

- *Why It's Essential*: Disability insurance provides income if you're unable to work due to illness or injury. Since a loss of income can impact your ability to pay for essentials, this type of insurance is crucial for financial stability.
- *Types of Disability Insurance*:
    - *Short-term disability*: Covers a portion of your income for a short period (usually 3–6 months).
    - *Long-term disability*: Provides coverage for a longer time, often until retirement age, if you experience a permanent or extended disability.
- *Choosing a Policy*: Consider a policy with coverage that meets your income needs. Evaluate the benefit period, elimination period (how long you wait before receiving benefits), and coverage amount. Employer-provided

plans are common, but supplemental private coverage may offer additional security.

3. Life Insurance: Providing for Loved Ones

- *Why It's Essential*: Life insurance offers financial support to your dependents if you pass away, helping cover expenses like funeral costs, debts, and ongoing living expenses. For families with children or individuals with significant debt, life insurance is often essential.
- *Types of Life Insurance*:
    - *Term Life*: Covers a specific term (e.g., 10, 20, or 30 years) and is generally more affordable. It's ideal for those wanting protection during key financial years (like while raising children).
    - *Whole Life*: Provides lifelong coverage and includes a cash value component that grows over time, making it more expensive but with potential for cash accumulation.
- *Choosing a Policy*: Determine how much coverage is needed based on your dependents' financial needs, your debts, and future expenses (like college costs for children). A term policy with sufficient coverage is often a cost-effective choice for many families.

4. Additional Insurance Types to Consider

- *Homeowners or Renters Insurance*: Protects your property and personal belongings, and can cover liability if someone is injured on your property.
- *Auto Insurance*: Covers accidents, damages, and liability in the event of a car accident, which is essential for financial protection if you drive.
- *Umbrella Insurance*: Provides additional liability coverage above and beyond standard policies, which can be useful for added protection if you have significant assets.

Choosing the Right Coverage for Your Needs

- Assess your life circumstances, dependents, and financial responsibilities to determine which policies are most relevant.
- Regularly review and update policies as your life changes (e.g., marriage, children, home ownership) to ensure coverage still meets your needs.
- Shop around for policies to compare premiums, coverage, and provider reliability.

By establishing insurance coverage that aligns with your life and goals, you'll have a financial safety net that helps protect you —and your loved ones—from the unexpected. The peace of mind that comes from having adequate insurance can be invaluable, especially in times of crisis.

Debt Management In Tough Times: Keeping Control When Challenges Arise

When financial setbacks lead to increased debt, effective debt management is essential for keeping it from spiraling out of control. This section provides strategies for managing debt wisely, reducing stress, and staying on track toward financial stability.

1. Prioritizing High-Interest Debt

- *Why Prioritize High-Interest Debt?* High-interest debt, like credit card balances, can quickly grow if left unpaid, thanks to compounding interest. Focusing on high-interest debt first minimizes the amount of money spent on interest over time, saving you money in the long run.
- *Debt Avalanche vs. Debt Snowball*:
    - *Debt Avalanche*: Pay off high-interest debts

first, then move to lower-interest debts. This approach minimizes overall interest costs.
    - *Debt Snowball*: Start with the smallest debt, regardless of interest rate, and pay it off first to build momentum. This approach can be motivating and may help build confidence, even if it costs more in interest.
- Choose the strategy that best fits your financial needs and psychological preferences. For many, the avalanche approach is financially efficient, while the snowball method offers quick wins.

2. Negotiating with Lenders

- *Why It Works*: Lenders often prefer to negotiate rather than risk non-payment. Negotiating can result in lower interest rates, reduced payments, or extended terms, making debt more manageable.
- *How to Negotiate*: Reach out to your lender, explain your situation, and inquire about options for temporary relief. Be polite but assertive, and have a clear sense of what you need to make payments sustainable.
- *Common Outcomes*: Some lenders may offer interest rate reductions, waive late fees, or allow smaller payments for a set period. Even a modest change can make a significant difference in managing your debt during tough times.

3. Understanding Deferment and Forbearance Options

- *Deferment and Forbearance Explained*: Deferment and forbearance temporarily pause or reduce loan payments, typically available on federal student loans and some types of private loans.
    - *Deferment*: Usually available for students or borrowers in specific situations (e.g., military service), this pauses both payments and

interest accrual in some cases.
- *Forbearance*: Allows for a temporary pause or reduction of payments, though interest often continues to accrue. This can be a short-term solution when you're facing hardship.
- *How to Apply*: Contact your lender, explain your financial situation, and ask about your options. You may need to provide documentation, such as proof of unemployment or financial hardship.

4. Debt Consolidation Options

- *What Is Debt Consolidation?* Debt consolidation combines multiple debts into a single loan, often with a lower interest rate or more manageable payment terms. This can simplify your payments and potentially save on interest.
- *Types of Consolidation*:
    - *Debt Consolidation Loan*: A personal loan used to pay off high-interest debts, which can reduce monthly payments or interest rates.
    - *Balance Transfer Credit Card*: Allows you to transfer high-interest credit card balances to a card with a lower introductory rate, often 0% for a specified period.
- *Is Consolidation Right for You?* Debt consolidation can be helpful if you qualify for lower interest rates and can commit to a repayment plan. However, it's important to avoid taking on additional debt after consolidation to prevent future challenges.

5. Seeking Support from Credit Counseling Services

- *Why Consider Credit Counseling?* Nonprofit credit counseling agencies can offer guidance on managing debt, creating a budget, and negotiating with creditors. Counselors may also help you set up a debt management

plan, where you make one monthly payment to the agency, which then distributes it to your creditors.
- *How to Find a Credible Agency*: Look for nonprofit credit counseling organizations accredited by the National Foundation for Credit Counseling (NFCC) or the Financial Counseling Association of America (FCAA). Be cautious of for-profit agencies, as some may charge high fees or engage in misleading practices.

6. Staying Focused on Financial Recovery

- *Budgeting and Tracking Progress*: Set a realistic budget that reflects your current circumstances and track your debt repayment progress regularly. Even small gains can help maintain motivation.
- *Avoiding New Debt*: Whenever possible, try to avoid new debt, especially high-interest options like payday loans. A focus on reducing existing debt rather than accumulating new liabilities will keep you on a path toward financial recovery.

By understanding and applying these debt management strategies, you can regain control over your finances even in tough times. The path may not always be easy, but small, consistent efforts will lead to big results over time, helping you emerge stronger and more financially resilient.

Staying Focused On Long-Term Financial Goals: Overcoming Setbacks With Resilience

Financial setbacks can disrupt plans and make it difficult to keep sight of long-term goals, but staying focused on the bigger picture is essential. Here are some strategies to help you stay committed, re-evaluate your goals as needed, and keep your motivation strong, even when times are tough.

1. Re-Evaluating and Adjusting Goals

    - *Assess Your Current Situation*: After a setback, take stock of your current financial position. Look at your budget, debt, savings, and any changes to your income. This assessment helps you make informed adjustments and see what's still within reach.
    - *Prioritize Goals Based on Current Needs*: Your financial priorities may shift due to changes in your situation. Identify which goals are still achievable and which may need modification. For instance, if paying off debt was your primary focus, you might now prioritize rebuilding an emergency fund.
    - *Set Realistic, Adjustable Milestones*: Break down your long-term goals into smaller, more manageable milestones. Setting short-term targets within a larger plan can keep you on track, even if you need to adjust timelines or contributions.

2. Keeping a Forward-Focused Mindset

    - *Remind Yourself of Your "Why"*: Think about the purpose behind your financial goals—whether it's a secure retirement, a down payment on a home, or a college fund for your children. Keeping your motivation in mind can strengthen your resolve to stay the course.
    - *Practice Positive Self-Talk*: Self-doubt and stress can creep in when facing setbacks. Practice affirmations and focus on the progress you've made rather than dwelling on setbacks. Acknowledge challenges, but remind yourself that you're capable of overcoming them.
    - *Stay Flexible and Adaptable*: Financial plans often require adjustments, especially during tough times. Accepting that change is part of the process allows you to adapt without feeling like you've "failed." Instead, view each adjustment as a step toward sustainable success.

3. Strategies for Staying Motivated

- *Celebrate Small Wins*: Every bit of progress counts. Whether it's paying down debt, saving a small amount each month, or hitting a new milestone, acknowledging these achievements can keep your motivation alive.
- *Track Your Progress*: Regularly review your goals and track any progress you've made, even if it's small. Tracking shows you that each step brings you closer to your goals and reinforces a sense of control over your finances.
- *Create Visual Reminders*: A vision board, financial goals tracker, or even sticky notes with your goals on them can help keep your goals front and center. Visual reminders help you stay focused and inspired during challenging periods.

4. Building Financial Resilience

- *Build an Emergency Plan*: Having a contingency plan for future setbacks can ease anxiety and give you the confidence to move forward. An emergency fund, insurance, or a backup budget can make a significant difference when unforeseen events arise.
- *Seek Accountability and Support*: Talk about your goals with a trusted friend, family member, or financial advisor. Sharing your plans can help you stay accountable and gain perspective, and others may offer encouragement or even practical advice for reaching your goals.
- *Reflect on Past Successes*: Look back at times when you overcame financial challenges. Reminding yourself of past resilience can help you believe in your ability to overcome current obstacles.

5. Focusing on Personal Growth During Tough Times

- *Expand Financial Knowledge*: Setbacks can be an opportunity to learn more about financial planning, budgeting, or investment. Increasing your financial literacy can provide you with tools to make better decisions and feel more in control of your journey.
- *Embrace Incremental Improvement*: Even small changes in your habits can make a big impact over time. Consider building or reinforcing positive financial habits like tracking expenses, setting up automated savings, or learning about low-risk investments.

Staying committed to long-term financial goals is about persistence, resilience, and a willingness to adapt. With these strategies, you can keep moving forward, confident that every small step and every adjustment brings you closer to the future you envision.

Stress Management And Financial Resilience: Navigating Tough Times With Strength

Financial setbacks can create significant stress, impacting not only your financial health but also your emotional well-being. Building financial resilience means developing the skills to manage stress effectively and maintain a positive outlook, even during challenging times. This chapter provides essential tips for managing financial stress, cultivating resilience, and prioritizing self-care as you navigate your financial journey.

1. Recognizing and Acknowledging Financial Stress

- *Identify Stress Triggers*: Take time to recognize what specific financial situations or decisions cause you

stress. This awareness can help you address those triggers more effectively.
- *Acknowledge Your Feelings*: It's normal to feel overwhelmed during financial difficulties. Acknowledging your feelings rather than suppressing them is the first step toward finding constructive solutions.

2. Developing a Financial Stress Management Plan

- *Create a Budget*: Having a clear budget can reduce uncertainty and help you gain control over your finances. Knowing where your money goes allows you to make informed decisions and plan for the future.
- *Break Tasks into Manageable Steps*: When facing a financial challenge, break the situation down into smaller, manageable tasks. For example, if you need to create a debt repayment plan, start by listing your debts and their interest rates, then prioritize them based on your chosen repayment strategy.

3. Cultivating Resilience

- *Develop a Growth Mindset*: Embrace the belief that challenges are opportunities for growth. Viewing setbacks as chances to learn and improve your financial skills can foster resilience and motivate you to take action.
- *Practice Problem-Solving Skills*: When facing a setback, focus on actionable solutions rather than getting bogged down by the problem. Brainstorm potential steps you can take to improve your situation and create a plan of action.

4. Prioritizing Self-Care

- *Incorporate Stress-Relief Techniques*: Engage in activities that help relieve stress, such as exercise, meditation, journaling, or spending time with loved ones. These practices can improve your mood and mental clarity, enabling you to make better financial decisions.
- *Set Boundaries with Financial Decisions*: If money-related discussions or situations are overwhelming, give yourself permission to step back. Taking breaks from stressful financial conversations can provide clarity and reduce anxiety.

5. Building a Support System

- *Reach Out for Support*: Don't hesitate to talk to friends, family, or professionals about your financial concerns. Sharing your experiences can alleviate feelings of isolation and provide valuable insights.
- *Consider Professional Help*: If financial stress feels unmanageable, consider working with a financial advisor or counselor. They can provide guidance tailored to your situation, helping you create a plan to move forward.

6. Fostering Long-Term Financial Resilience

- *Establish an Emergency Fund*: Having a financial cushion can significantly reduce stress during emergencies. Aim to save at least three to six months' worth of living expenses to prepare for unexpected challenges.
- *Educate Yourself Financially*: Continuously learning about personal finance, budgeting, and investment can enhance your confidence in managing money. Knowledge is a powerful tool that can help you make informed decisions.

7. Embracing a Positive Perspective

- *Focus on What You Can Control*: In times of uncertainty, concentrate on aspects of your financial situation you can influence, such as budgeting, spending habits, or savings strategies.
- *Celebrate Progress, No Matter How Small*: Acknowledge your efforts and celebrate milestones, even if they seem minor. Recognizing progress reinforces motivation and encourages you to keep moving forward.

Conclusion: Bouncing Back With Confidence

By learning to anticipate, prepare for, and bounce back from financial setbacks, you'll build the resilience needed to navigate life's challenges with confidence. Remember that financial resilience is not just about managing money; it's about handling the emotional impact of setbacks and prioritizing your overall well-being. With the right mindset and strategies, you can face financial challenges head-on, emerging stronger and more equipped for whatever comes next.

CHAPTER 10: CELEBRATING THE THOUSANDAIRE MILESTONE

Building on Your Financial Success

Reaching the status of a thousandaire—having at least $1,000 in savings or assets or creating an additional $1000 a month in disposable income—is a significant achievement in your financial journey. It represents a solid foundation upon which you can build further success. This final chapter will discuss how to celebrate this milestone, maintain your financial progress, and leverage your accomplishments to achieve future goals, whether that's becoming debt-free, saving for a house, or continuing on the path to millionaire status.

1. Celebrate Your Achievement

- *Acknowledge Your Hard Work*: Take a moment to recognize the effort and discipline that led you to this milestone. Celebrate your commitment to saving

and managing your finances. Consider sharing your achievement with family and friends to reinforce your success and inspire others.
- *Treat Yourself Mindfully*: Consider treating yourself to something meaningful that doesn't compromise your financial stability. This could be a small celebration, a nice meal, or a day out that reinforces your commitment to enjoying the journey without overspending.

2. Review Your Financial Situation

- *Assess Your Current Finances*: Take stock of your financial situation, including your savings, expenses, debts, and overall net worth. Understanding where you stand is crucial as you plan for your next steps.
- *Revisit Your Goals*: Reflect on your short-term and long-term financial goals. Evaluate if they still align with your values and priorities. This reassessment can help you stay focused and motivated as you move forward.

3. Strengthen Your Emergency Fund

- *Build on Your Savings*: If you've reached the $1,000 mark, consider setting a new savings target for your emergency fund. Aim for three to six months' worth of expenses, providing a solid cushion for unexpected situations.
- *Automate Future Contributions*: Continue contributing to your emergency fund through automatic transfers. Automating your savings will make it easier to maintain your progress and ensure you don't forget to prioritize this important goal.

4. Tackle Debt Strategically

- *Evaluate Your Debt Situation*: If you have existing debts, now is the time to take a close look at them. Determine which debts are high-interest and prioritize them in your repayment strategy.
- *Create a Debt Repayment Plan*: Develop a structured plan for paying off debt. Whether you choose the debt avalanche or snowball method, stay committed to making regular payments and reducing your debt burden.

5. Set New Financial Goals

- *Identify Your Next Milestones*: With a solid foundation established, consider what comes next. This could include saving for a home, increasing your investment portfolio, or even aiming for the millionaire status.
- *Create a Savings and Investment Strategy*: Develop a plan that outlines how you'll achieve your new goals. This could involve setting aside a certain percentage of your income for savings or investments, contributing to retirement accounts, or exploring additional income streams.

6. Invest in Yourself

- *Enhance Your Financial Literacy*: Continue to educate yourself about personal finance, investment strategies, and wealth-building. Knowledge is a powerful tool that will serve you well as you navigate your financial journey.
- *Consider Professional Guidance*: If your goals become more complex, consider consulting with a financial advisor. They can provide personalized advice and strategies to help you reach your objectives effectively.

7. Cultivate a Wealth-Building Mindset

- *Adopt a Growth Mindset*: Embrace the belief that you can continue to improve your financial situation. Stay open to learning, adapting, and seeking opportunities for growth.
- *Focus on Consistency*: Remember that building wealth is a marathon, not a sprint. Stay consistent in your saving and investing efforts, and don't be discouraged by setbacks. Small, regular contributions can lead to significant results over time.

Conclusion: The Path Forward

Reaching the thousandaire milestone is a cause for celebration, and it serves as a vital stepping stone toward greater financial success. By recognizing your achievement, assessing your situation, and setting new goals, you can continue to build on this foundation. As you embark on the next phase of your financial journey, remember that each step you take brings you closer to your long-term aspirations. Stay committed, stay informed, and celebrate the progress you make along the way—because every milestone, no matter how small, is a testament to your dedication to achieving financial security and success.

Conclusion: Becoming a thousandaire is not just about hitting a specific number—it's about developing the habits, discipline, and mindset to achieve lasting financial security. This book has outlined the steps and strategies to help you start your journey to financial independence. Remember, building wealth isn't about making huge leaps, but about taking consistent, smart steps forward.

ABOUT THE AUTHOR

David Runyon

David (Dave) Runyon is an entrepreneur and small business owner. With a background in Environmental Engineering and Consulting, he spent nearly 25 years as a regional manager as well as President and CEO of two environmental firms. He has also had "Thousandaire" success in multiple network marketing companies including  becoming a six-figure earner. He also had several successful small business "Side Hustles" thru the years. At the time of publishing this book, he was in the men's clothing and formal wear retail industry.

www.ingramcontent.com/pod-product-compliance
Lightning Source LLC
Chambersburg PA
CBHW070253220526
45465CB00004B/1600